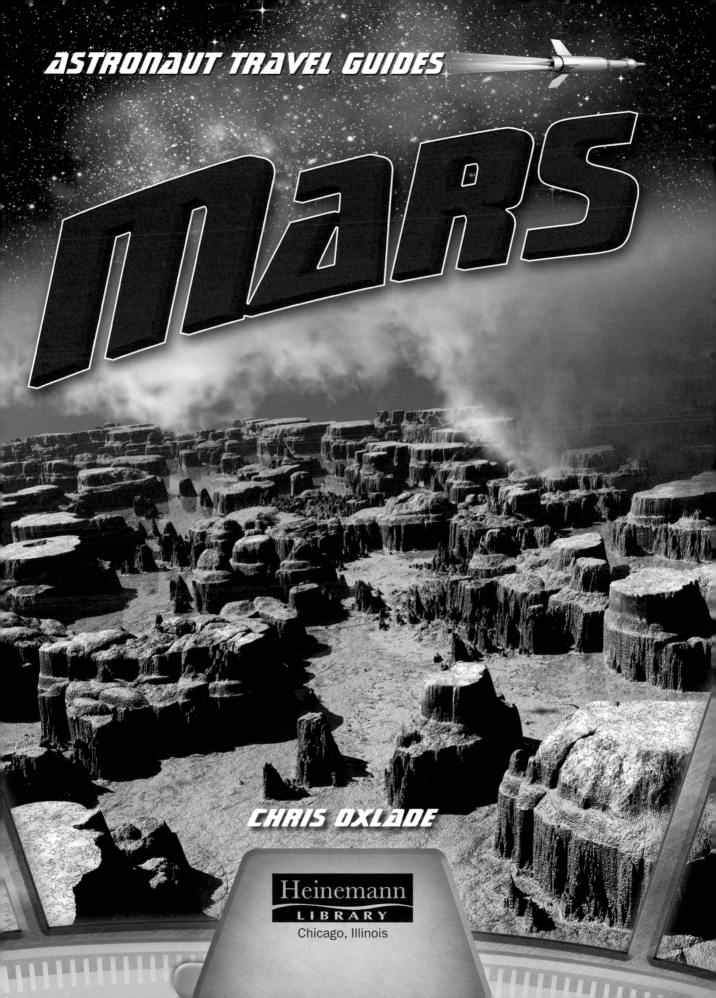

www.capstonepub.com
Visit our website to find out
more information about
Heinemann-Raintree books.

To order:
☎ Phone 800-747-4992
📠 Visit www.capstonepub.com
to browse our catalog and order online.

Edited by Nancy Dickmann and Laura Knowles
Designed by Steve Mead
Original illustrations © Capstone Global
Library Ltd 2013
Picture research by Mica Brancic

Originated by Capstone Global Library Ltd
Printed and bound in the United States of
America in North Mankato, MN.
012013   007120RP

16 15 14 13
10 9 8 7 6 5 4 3 2

Library of Congress Cataloging-in-
Publication Data
Oxlade, Chris.
Mars / Chris Oxlade.—1st ed.
p. cm.—(Astronaut travel guides)
Includes bibliographical references and index.
ISBN 978-1-4109-4570-9 (hb)—ISBN 978-1-
4109-4579-2 (pb) 1. Mars (Planet)—Juvenile
literature. I. Title.
QB641.095 2013
523.43—dc23   2011038995

Acknowledgements
We would like to thank the following for
permission to reproduce photographs: © Corbis
p. 31; © European Space Agency p. 25 (IBMP/O.
Voloshin); p. 16 (S. Corvaja, 2011); Gary Bross
p. 6; Getty Images p. 7 (De Agostini Picture
Library/G Dagli Orti); NASA pp. 4 (The Hubble
Heritage Team (STScI/AURA)), 9 (G. Neukum
(FU Berlin) et al., Mars Express, DLR, ESA), 11
(NSSDC), 5 top and 13, 14 (JPL), 18 (JPL/Arizona
State University), 19 (Goddard Space Flight
Center/Scientific Visualization Studio), 21 (JPL/
USGS), 24 (ESA), 28, 5 middle and 29 (Langley
Research Center/Sean Smith), 30 (Goddard
Space Flight Center Scientific Visualization
Studio), 34 (JPL-Caltech), 15 (JPL-Caltech); Rex
Features p. 22 (Everett Collection); Science
Photo Library pp. 8 (Detlev Van Ravenswaay),
23 (NASA), 26 (RIA Novosti), 36 (Walter Myers),
38 (European Space Agency); Scott Maxwell
pp. 5 bottom and 32; Shutterstock pp. 40-41
(© Martiin || Fluidworkshop).

Design image elements reproduced with
permission of Shutterstock/© Jan Kaliciak/
© Spectral-Design/© Stephen Girimont/© yexelA

Cover photograph of the surface of Mars
reproduced with permission of Shutterstock/
© Dariush M.

We would like to thank Scott Maxwell for his
invaluable help in the preparation of this book.

CONTENTS

Some words are shown in bold, **like this**. You can find out what they mean by looking in the glossary.

DON'T FORGET

These boxes will remind you what you need to take with you on your big adventure.

NUMBER CRUNCHING

Don't miss these little chunks of data as you speed through the travel guide!

AMAZING FACTS

You need to know these fascinating facts to get the most out of your space safari!

WHO'S WHO?

Find out about the space explorers who have studied the universe in the past and today.

DESTINATION MARS

Have you ever seen Mars in the night sky? It is a big planet, but from Earth it looks like a small red dot. Mars is the fourth planet from the Sun, and it is the planet in the **solar system** most like Earth. Nobody has been to Mars yet. But it will be the first planet that astronauts visit. Are you ready for the trip?

Through a **telescope**, we can see patches of light and dark on Mars and ice at the **poles**.

WHY VISIT MARS?

There are plenty of good reasons to visit Mars. Scientists want to find out more about Mars—about its rocks, its weather, and its volcanoes, **canyons**, and **ice caps**. They also want to find out whether there is, or was, life on Mars. Of course, you might want to go to Mars just to see the amazing sights and to explore its landscape.

We know lots about Mars from the space **probes** that have visited the planet. But human visitors could find out much more. On the downside, it would be a dangerous, long, and expensive journey. And, at the moment, we do not have the spacecraft to make it.

See pages 12–13 to find out about robots on Mars!

Find out what equipment you will need on Mars on pages 28–29.

Meet Mars **rover** driver Scott Maxwell on pages 32–35.

AMAZING FACTS

Today, the surface of Mars is a cold, dry, and dusty place. But evidence from Martian rocks, and features such as dry **channels** in the surface, show us that liquid water once flowed on Mars. Billions of years ago, Mars may have been more like Earth is today!

Mars appears in the night sky as a bright red star (the light from Mars is sunlight bouncing off it). In ancient times, **astronomers** (people who study space) saw that Mars moved across the background of stars, so they knew it was a planet rather than a star. Hundreds of years later, astronomers first studied Mars with telescopes. Since the 1960s, many robotic spacecraft have visited the planet.

Mars is a bright red spot in the night sky. It looks brightest when it is on the same side of the Sun as Earth.

MARS AND THE GODS

In ancient Greece and ancient Rome, Mars was linked with war because it is the color of blood. It was named after Mars, the Roman god of war. In Greece, Mars was linked with Ares, the Greek god of war. Around 3,000 years ago, Babylonian astronomers called the planet Nergal, after their god of death and disease.

MARS MOVEMENTS

Seen from Earth, Mars normally moves in one direction across the background of stars. But sometimes it moves the other way. Early astronomers could not understand this movement. In the 1500s, Danish astronomer Tycho Brahe made careful observations of Mars. German astronomer Johannes Kepler used Brahe's work to discover that Mars **orbits** the Sun in a crushed circle, which explained the peculiar movement.

Mars was the Roman god of war. He was also the protector of Rome and the guardian of the ruler of Rome, the emperor. The month of March is named after Mars, and that is when Romans held festivals in his honor.

Mars was one of the most important Roman gods.

DISCOVERIES WITH TELESCOPES

The first telescopes were made in the 1600s. Astronomers soon pointed them at the night sky. One of them, the Italian Galileo Galilei, looked at Mars and saw a disc rather than a tiny point of light, proving that it was a planet rather than a star. Dutchman Christiaan Huygens sketched its dark and light areas.

In 1877, Italian astronomer Giovanni Schiaparelli made sketches of Mars that were more detailed than any before. He drew dark lines that he described as channels, or *canali* in Italian. This was mistaken for "canal," and before long there was talk of Martians digging canals. When space probes arrived at Mars in the 1960s, there were no canals—Schiaparelli had seen an **optical illusion**.

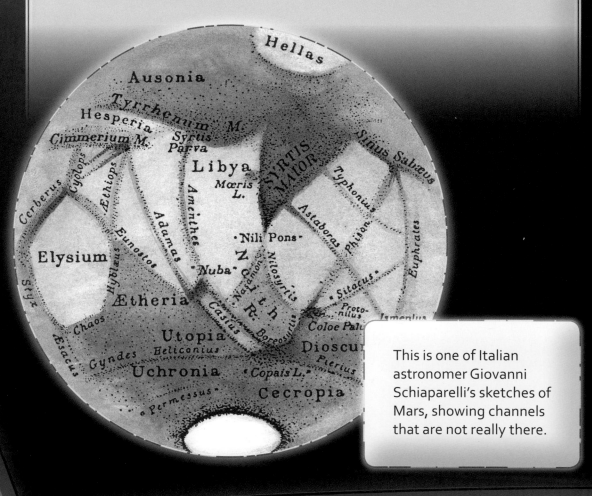

This is one of Italian astronomer Giovanni Schiaparelli's sketches of Mars, showing channels that are not really there.

MARS'S MOONS DISCOVERED

Mars has two small, potato-shaped moons. Asaph Hall, a U.S. astronomer working at the U.S. Naval Observatory, discovered them in 1877. He named them Phobos and Deimos, from Greek words for "fear" and "terror."

This is Phobos, the larger of the two Martian moons. It is 17 miles (27 kilometers) long and 13 miles (21 kilometers) wide.

WHO'S WHO?

Christiaan Huygens (1629–1695) was a Dutch mathematician and astronomer. He spent much of his life in Paris, France, where he studied. Huygens made his own telescopes, which allowed him to see more detail on the planets than other astronomers. He discovered that Mars spins on its **axis** once about every 24 hours, like Earth, and that Saturn's rings are circular.

PROBES TO MARS

More than 30 robot spacecraft, called probes, have already visited Mars. Probes either fly past a planet (a visit known as a flyby), orbit the planet, or land on the planet. Many Mars probes have been lost almost as soon as they got to the planet—or even before they arrived—including the **European Space Agency's lander**, called *Beagle*, in 2003.

MARINER AT MARS

The first successful probe to arrive at Mars was *Mariner 4*, in 1965. Scientists were disappointed that photographs from *Mariner 4* showed a dead world, like the Moon. *Mariner 6* and *Mariner 7* followed in 1969, and they sent more detailed images. In 1971, *Mariner 9* went into orbit around Mars. It sent back more than 7,300 images of the Martian surface, including pictures of volcanoes, which amazed scientists.

NUMBER CRUNCHING

The probe *Mariner 4* took a long eight months to travel from Earth to Mars. As it hurtled past Mars, it had just 20 minutes to take photographs. Probe-to-Earth communications were very slow in 1965, and it took three weeks for *Mariner 4* to send the photographs back to Earth by radio.

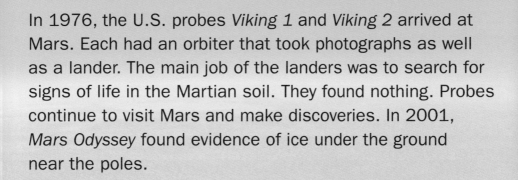

In 1976, the U.S. probes *Viking 1* and *Viking 2* arrived at Mars. Each had an orbiter that took photographs as well as a lander. The main job of the landers was to search for signs of life in the Martian soil. They found nothing. Probes continue to visit Mars and make discoveries. In 2001, *Mars Odyssey* found evidence of ice under the ground near the poles.

This photograph of Mars was taken by *Viking 2*, which has taken a soil sample from the surface.

NUMBER CRUNCHING

Mars rovers are controlled by radio signals from Earth. The signals travel at the speed of light, but Mars is so far away that it still takes them up to 20 minutes to arrive. Images from the rovers' cameras take the same time to reach Earth. The rovers' movements are programmed in advance, because there is such a long time gap between sending a command and seeing the results.

ROVING ON MARS

A lander stays in one place, but a **rover** can explore more of the planet. **NASA's** Mars Pathfinder was the first probe with a rover to visit Mars. It landed in 1997. The six-wheeled rover was called Sojourner. It traveled to several rocks and investigated them, and it also took hundreds of photographs. In 2004, rovers called Spirit and Opportunity landed on opposite sides of Mars to search for signs of water. They have found rocks that appear to have been underwater a long time ago.

AMAZING FACTS

In 2011, the Opportunity rover was still on Mars and sending back important information—seven years after it landed. Overall, it has traveled more than 21 miles (34 kilometers) over the Martian surface. Spirit malfunctioned in 2010, and scientists have been unable to "wake" it up.

The *Mars Curiosity* probe (also known as the Mars Science Laboratory) launched in November 2011. Its main job will be to collect rock samples by drilling into rocks. It will also check levels of harmful **radiation** on Mars to get an idea of the dangers that will face future astronauts.

Mars Curiosity carries a laser that will vaporize rocks, so that its sensors can analyze them.

MARS SCIENCE

Before a visit to Mars, you will need to know a few facts about the planet. Nobody has ever visited Mars; what we know about it comes from observations from Earth and from space probes (see page 10). Like Earth, Mars was formed from pieces of rock left over after the Sun was formed.

MARS VS. EARTH

Mars's orbit is like a crushed circle. At its closest it is about 129 million miles (208 million kilometers) from the Sun. At its farthest it is 155 million miles (249 million kilometers) from the Sun. A day on Mars lasts just over 24 hours.

The **diameter** (width) of Mars (right) is a little over half the diameter of Earth (left).

GRAVITY ON MARS

Gravity is the force that pulls objects together. On Earth, it pulls you toward the ground. On Mars, it would pull you down to the surface of Mars. Because Mars is much smaller than Earth, its gravity is only about one-third as strong as Earth's gravity. So if you stood on Mars, the force pulling you down would be only one-third as strong as on Earth. It also means that objects would be easier to lift on Mars.

DIAMETER:
4,220 miles (6,792 kilometers)

MASS (COMPARED TO EARTH):
10 percent of Earth's **mass**

AVERAGE DISTANCE FROM SUN:
141,635,996 miles
(227,941,040 kilometers)

AVERAGE SURFACE TEMPERATURE:
-82 °Fahrenheit (-63 °Celsius)

GRAVITY:
0.38 times Earth gravity

After the Sun was formed, material left over drifted together because of gravity to form Mars and the other planets.

HOW FAR TO MARS?

The distance between Earth and Mars changes as the planets orbit the Sun. When both planets are on the same side of the Sun, Mars is less than 35 million miles (56 million kilometers) away. But when it is on the other side of the Sun, it is nearly 250 million miles (400 million kilometers) away.

You will need a powerful rocket to escape Earth's gravity and travel to Mars.

DON'T FORGET

Expect to be stuck in a small spacecraft drifting through space for many months as you travel to Mars and back again. There will be jobs to do, but lots of spare time. So don't forget to take something to entertain yourself, such as video games and plenty of books to read.

STRAIGHT AND CURVED PATHS

Flying straight from Earth to Mars when the planets are closest together might take a few weeks in a spacecraft. But you would have to fire a rocket engine, using lots and lots of fuel, to slow down and stop when you arrive at Mars. A much better route is a curved path. After leaving Earth, you coast through space, slowly catching up with Mars. This means burning only a little fuel to slow down and match speed with Mars.

There are two problems with taking a curved route. First, you can only go when the planets are in just the right position, and that only happens every couple of years. Second, the route is a long one, and it takes about nine months to get there.

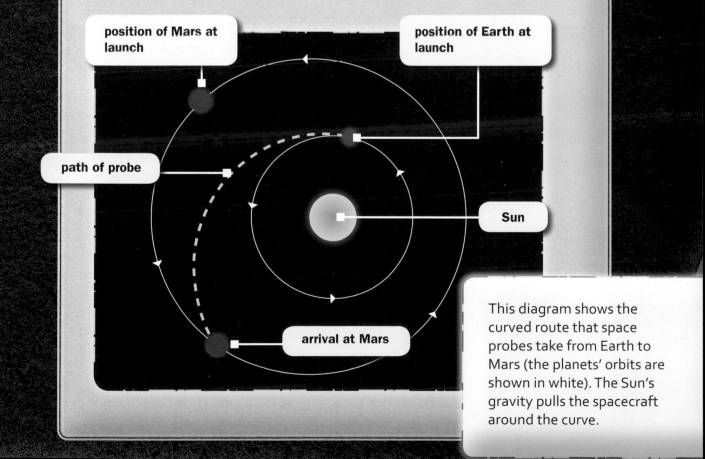

position of Mars at launch

position of Earth at launch

path of probe

Sun

arrival at Mars

This diagram shows the curved route that space probes take from Earth to Mars (the planets' orbits are shown in white). The Sun's gravity pulls the spacecraft around the curve.

MARS ROCK

The surface of Mars is covered with red-brown rocks and dust. The color comes from a mineral called iron oxide (commonly known as rust) in the rock, and it is why Mars is known as the Red Planet. There are huge dark and light areas on the surface, which are made up of rocks of slightly different colors. The largest dark area is called Syrtis Major.

SURFACE FEATURES

The surface of Mars's northern **hemisphere** and its southern hemisphere are very different. The northern hemisphere is made up of low, flat plains, with very few **craters**. The southern hemisphere is high and covered with craters. There are many interesting features on the surface at the boundary between the hemispheres, including valleys, channels, ridges, and volcanoes.

The probe *Mars Odyssey* took this photograph of the Martian volcano called Hecates Tholus. The volcano is 114 miles (183 kilometers) across.

The Tharsis Rise is a huge volcanic dome that rises about 6 miles (10 kilometers) above the northern plains. On its top are three huge volcanoes. Close by is the solar system's biggest known volcano, Olympus Mons. It is more than twice as high as Mount Everest. Around the **equator** is a huge system of canyons known as the Valles Marineris. It is more than 2,485 miles (4,000 kilometers) long, and it is up to 6 miles (9 kilometers) deep.

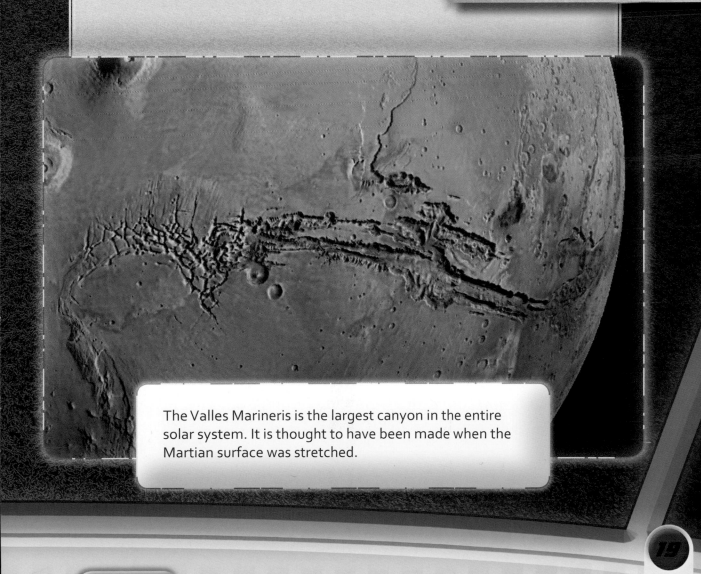

The Valles Marineris is the largest canyon in the entire solar system. It is thought to have been made when the Martian surface was stretched.

MARS'S ATMOSPHERE

Like Earth, Mars has an **atmosphere** of gases around it. But Mars's atmosphere is thinner than Earth's. It is made mostly of a gas called carbon dioxide. There is no oxygen for astronauts to breathe. In comparison, Earth's atmosphere is mostly nitrogen and oxygen.

The **water vapor** in Mars's atmosphere sometimes turns to tiny ice crystals, which form thin clouds above the surface over the poles and form fog in the craters and canyons. The atmosphere is heated by the Sun, making the gases swirl around, creating winds.

SEASONS AND ICE CAPS

The axis of Mars is tilted a little, just like the axis of Earth. Different parts of the surface are heated by different amounts as Mars orbits the Sun. This creates seasons, just like the seasons on Earth. In winter in the northern hemisphere, an ice cap grows at the north pole. Water vapor and carbon dioxide from the atmosphere form water ice and carbon dioxide ice. The ice melts away again in the summer. The ice cap at the south pole is always there. It grows larger during winter and gets smaller in summer.

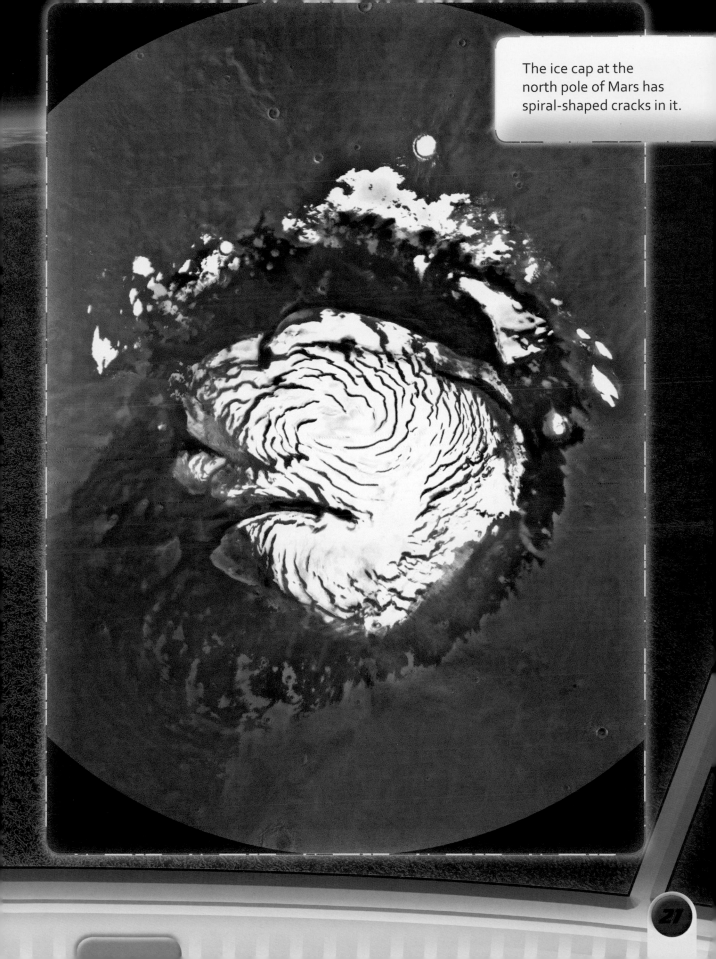

The ice cap at the north pole of Mars has spiral-shaped cracks in it.

LIFE ON MARS

Is there life on Mars? Before the first probes visited Mars, people thought there could be some form of life on Mars. The search for life, or evidence of life in the past, is a major reason for sending astronauts to Mars. Today, Mars appears to be a dead world. But in the distant past, water flowed on the surface.

AMAZING FACTS

Many science-fiction writers have written about Martians. They include H. G. Wells, who wrote *War of the Worlds*, which was published in 1898. The story was about a terrifying Martian invasion. In 1938, a radio play of the novel caused panic in parts of the United States. Thousands of people thought there was a real invasion taking place.

War of the Worlds has been filmed several times. This is a poster for the 1953 version.

LOOKING FOR LIFE

The *Viking* spacecraft that landed on Mars in 1976 searched for signs of life in the Martian soil, but it found nothing. But scientists have not given up. The latest probes are also searching for signs of life in the soil. You could also search for life on a mission to Mars.

AMAZING FACTS

A **meteorite** found in Antarctica in 1984 was one of many that came from Mars. This one was called ALH 84001. Seen under a microscope, it appeared to contain **fossils** of **microorganisms**. It caused excitement at the time, but most experts now think the "fossils" were just tiny rock formations.

This is the famous meteorite ALH 84001, which came from Mars and was once thought to contain fossils of Martian life.

PLANNING YOUR TRIP

There are plenty of details to be decided before you set out for Mars. What sort of spacecraft would you need? Who would you take with you, and what equipment? When would you go, and where would you land?

Astronauts stay aboard the **International Space Station** for months on end. A trip to Mars would take at least a year.

A SUITABLE SPACECRAFT

At the moment, no spacecraft exists that is suitable for a human mission to Mars. You would need a spacecraft big enough to carry you, your fellow astronauts, and all the equipment and supplies you would need for a year-long trip. The craft would need to protect you from harmful radiation in space and provide you with oxygen to breathe. The spacecraft would be too big to be launched from Earth at one time, so it would be assembled bit by bit in Earth's orbit.

WHEN TO GO

You can only set off when Earth and Mars are in suitable positions in their orbits (see page 16). That only happens once every couple of years. When you arrive, you would probably land wherever it is summer on Mars, so your stay would be warmer and lighter.

AMAZING FACTS

You will be spending months in a cramped space with other astronauts. You will have to do some training to make sure you would cope. In 2010–2011, astronauts from the European Space Agency and Russian MARS-500 project underwent a pretend Mars mission. They spent more than 500 days living in a mock-up spacecraft to see how they performed. They even performed practice spacewalks on a pretend Martian surface.

After more than a year, the MARS-500 crew members came out of their "spaceship" in November 2011.

WHO'S GOING WITH YOU?

You will be traveling to Mars with other astronauts. Who would your ideal traveling companions be? Remember that you will have to get along well with them—it is a long way in a small spacecraft! Here are some ideas to get you thinking.

CREW MEMBER:

VALERI POLYAKOV (BORN 1942)
Polyakov was a Russian doctor who trained to be an astronaut. In 1994, he flew to the Mir **Space Station** and stayed there for 438 days. It is the longest-ever stay in space.

POTENTIAL JOB:
Mission commander

CREW MEMBER:

ERNEST SHACKLETON (1874–1922)
Shackleton made three trips to the Antarctic at the beginning of the 1900s. On the second trip, he nearly reached the South Pole by sled. On the third, he led his men to safety after their ship was crushed by ice floes.

POTENTIAL JOB:
Investigating the Martian poles

CREW MEMBER:

GIOVANNI SCHIAPARELLI (1835–1910)

Schiaparelli was an Italian astronomer. In 1877, he thought he saw thin channels on Mars. He would be amazed to see real giant canyons on Mars.

POTENTIAL JOB:

Photographer and artist

CREW MEMBER:

SCIENCE TEACHER

Perhaps your science teacher would enjoy a trip to Mars. He or she could teach you all about Mars and the science of space and space flight. There will be plenty of time to listen!

POTENTIAL JOB:

Mission teacher

CREW MEMBER:

VOLCANOLOGIST

Giant volcanoes are on Mars. Any volcanologist (person who studies volcanoes) would love to climb Olympus Mons, the biggest volcano in the solar system.

POTENTIAL JOB:

Investigating the Martian volcanoes

You will need to stay healthy and fit during your Mars mission. So there will be an exercise machine on board that you will need to use every day. Exercise will keep your muscles in shape for when you walk on Mars or Earth after months in **zero gravity**.

Astronauts on the International Space Station exercise for at least two hours a day.

EQUIPMENT FOR MARS

You will need a huge amount of equipment for any mission to Mars. This includes items such as your clothes, your spacesuit (see below), your hygiene kit (toothbrush, toothpaste, and cleaning wipes), and all your food. You will get three meals a day, pre-packed in pouches, with some of it dried.

You will be allowed to take some personal equipment to make the trip more enjoyable. You might have some hard choices to make, because you cannot take much with you. There will be a strict weight limit—perhaps 22 pounds (10 kilograms) per person. But don't bring your cell phone— there will not be a signal in space or on Mars!

CLOTHES

On board your spacecraft you will just need some loose, comfortable clothing for everyday wear. To go outside on Mars, you will need a spacesuit. This complex suit will protect you from harmful rays from space, regulate your temperature, and provide you with oxygen to breathe.

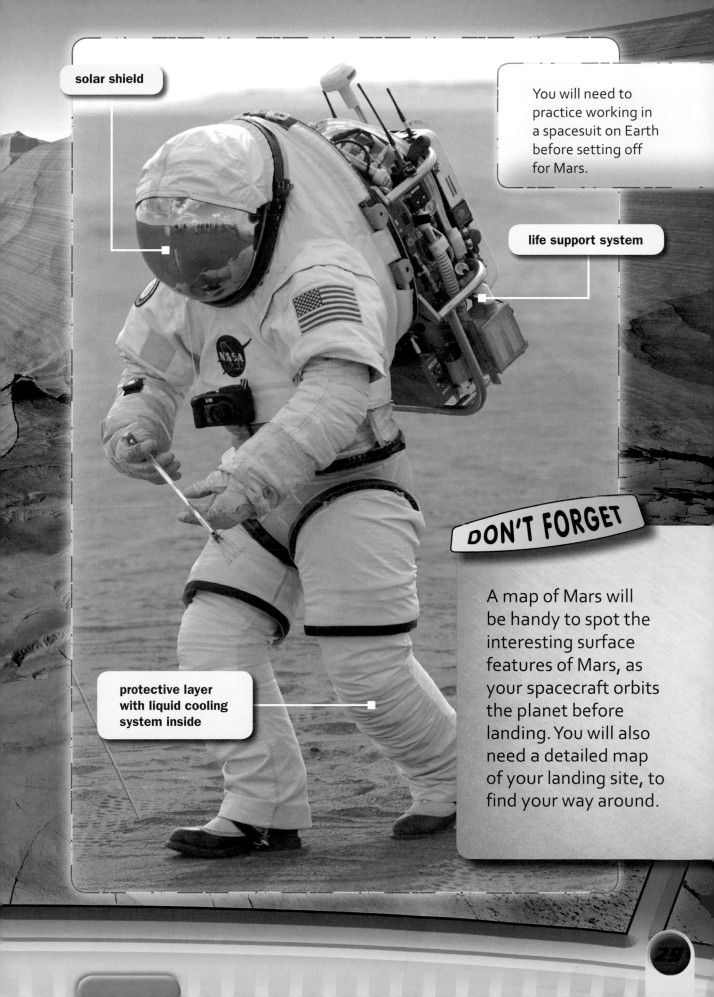

solar shield

You will need to practice working in a spacesuit on Earth before setting off for Mars.

life support system

protective layer with liquid cooling system inside

DON'T FORGET

A map of Mars will be handy to spot the interesting surface features of Mars, as your spacecraft orbits the planet before landing. You will also need a detailed map of your landing site, to find your way around.

THINGS TO SEE ON MARS

There are amazing sights to see all over Mars. New ones are being discovered by probes all the time. You might land near one of these features, or you might travel by rover to see one.

Here are the locations of some of the sites mentioned on these pages.

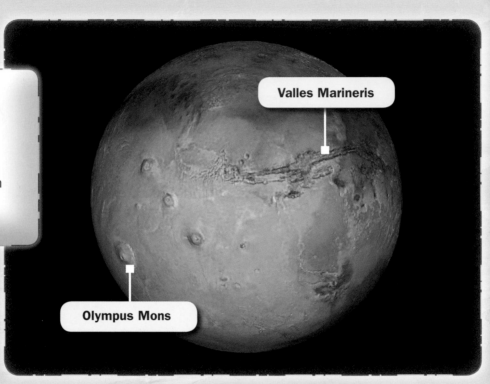

Valles Marineris

Olympus Mons

Valles Marineris

The giant canyon system Valles Marineris stretches over 2,485 miles (4,000 kilometers) around the Martian equator. It is five times as deep as the Grand Canyon on Earth.

The ice caps

Visit either of the poles and you will find ice on the ground. Visit in the fall or spring and you will see the caps growing or shrinking as the temperature falls or rises.

Olympus Mons

The giant volcano of Olympus Mons stands 13 miles (21 kilometers) high. At its base, it is 335 miles (540 kilometers) across. Visit the summit (highest point) and you will see a crater 53 miles (85 kilometers) across. Olympus Mons could be one billion years old.

While in orbit above Mars, you will see the Olympus Mons, a giant volcano.

Landers and rovers

For a little space exploration history, you could visit the sites where probes have landed in the past. The probes will still be there. The most famous are the historic *Viking* landers and the rovers *Spirit* and *Opportunity*.

DON'T FORGET

You will probably want to bring some Mars rock back to Earth, to share with scientists. It will be very rare back on Earth, because the only other Martian rock on Earth comes from meteorites.

INTERVIEW WITH A ROVER DRIVER

Scott Maxwell works for NASA's Jet Propulsion Laboratory as a rover driver. His team controls the *Spirit* and *Opportunity* rovers that explore the surface of Mars.

Q *What kinds of controllers do you use to drive the rovers?*

A Well, we wish we had something like a computer game control pad. But even when Earth and Mars are close to each other, it takes four minutes for a signal you send to get to Mars, and another four minutes for signals to return. So if we pushed forward on our joystick, it would take four minutes before the rover heard it was supposed to move, and then another four minutes before we found out what it was doing. When Earth and Mars are farther apart, the delay goes up to 20 minutes each way. By the time you see the cliff coming, you've already gone over it!

The rovers are solar-powered and they shut down for the Martian night. So when it's late afternoon on Mars, the rovers stop and send us pictures and other data about the world around them. Then they go to sleep, and my team and I go to work.

We make the data into a 3-D world—like a video game—that runs on our computers. We put a software copy of the rover down in that world and send it commands, and it responds in much the same way the real rover would. We plan out the rover's next day, so that when it wakes up again, there is a new list of commands for it to carry out.

Q Are there other difficulties in controlling something so far away?

A A Martian day is almost 40 minutes longer than an Earth day. A solar-powered rover only works when the Sun is up in the Martian sky, so we work on the Mars clock. For the first three months of the mission, we matched up with Mars time by coming in to work at 8 o'clock one day, 8:40 the next day, then at 9:20, and so on. Pretty soon you're coming in to work at wacky times like 2 o'clock in the morning!

Q What do you think is the most interesting thing the rovers have found so far?

A Both rovers have found good surface evidence that Mars was once a very different planet from today. Today, Mars is a miserable, frozen, nearly airless desert, but it wasn't always so. In the distant past, Mars was warmer and wetter, with a thicker atmosphere. Not only does this mean that life once had a chance there—whether it ever started there or not—but it also tells us that dramatic changes like that can happen to planets.

Q What will the next generation of rovers be like?

A We've already built the next Mars rover—the Mars Science Laboratory (nicknamed "*Curiosity*")—and we launched it in November 2011. It will do a better job of looking inside things. But the most exciting thing is that it has a laser on its head. It can burn holes in rocks! This means that you can find out from a distance what the rocks are made of, without having to go over and explore each one up close.
I just think it's fun to shoot a laser on Mars!

This illustration shows what *Mars Curiosity* will look like when it uses its powerful laser.

Q *Rovers have already visited Mars and Earth's Moon. Do you think we will ever use rovers on another planet or moon, and if so, which one?*

A Saturn's moon Titan and Jupiter's moon Europa are two good places, although it might be more appropriate to send boats or submarines there. Titan is partly covered with methane lakes, and Europa is an ice ball with liquid below the surface, making a submarine a good choice there.

Q *Do you have any space heroes?*

A Neil Armstrong is an all-time personal favorite, both for his accomplishment of being the first human on the Moon and for his upstanding personal behavior. The Mars Exploration Rover Mission's chief scientist, Steve Squyres, is not only a great communicator and amazing to work with, but just a super-nice guy. Among robots, my long-time heroes are the *Voyager* probes. They were the first robots ever to explore the outer planets.

Q *If you had the opportunity, which planets (or other space bodies) would you like to visit in person, and why?*

A All of them! I'd go to the stars! But if I had to pick just one, it would be Mars. It's a planet I know pretty well at this point—and I have a couple of robot friends there that I would dearly love to visit.

STAYING ON MARS

How difficult and dangerous is it to stay on the surface of Mars? Could you survive for a short stay of a few weeks or months? What about staying on Mars many months or even years, at a permanent base? For a short stay, you could take everything you need (oxygen, water, and food), but for a long stay, you would need to find resources on Mars.

This is what it might look like if astronauts lived and worked on Mars.

Mars is a cold place. The average temperature is around −82 degrees Fahrenheit (−63 degrees Celsius), which is too cold for humans to survive, although it can reach a pleasant 62 degrees Fahrenheit (17 degrees Celsius) on summer days. Radiation is your greatest enemy on Mars. The long-term effects of radiation need to be researched before any astronaut goes to Mars.

DON'T FORGET

A Mars day is 36 Earth minutes longer than an Earth day. An Earth clock would quickly get out of time with the Mars day and night. So you might want a Mars-time clock to wake you up in the morning!

NUMBER CRUNCHING

You could not leave Mars whenever you wanted. You would have to wait until Mars and Earth were in the right places in their orbits. If you traveled there using as little fuel as possible (taking 8 months to reach Mars), you would have to stay for around 15 months before you could leave again. But if you used a "high-energy" route, using lots of fuel, you could leave after a month or two.

MARS BASE

A permanent Mars base would need living space, storage space for equipment and supplies, and a science laboratory. It would need to create a safe environment for you to survive in. Robot spacecraft would probably transport the parts of the base and supplies to Mars before astronauts set off.

This is the European Space Agency's idea of what a permanent Mars base could be like in the future.

Supply trips from Earth would be few and far between. Your oxygen and water would be recycled as much as possible (water can even be recycled from your urine). There is plenty of ice underground on Mars. This could be mined for water supplies. Splitting the water into oxygen and hydrogen could provide oxygen to breathe and hydrogen for fuel.

PLANS FOR MARS

It will be many years before astronauts can live on Mars. However, several space agencies, including NASA, the European Space Agency, and the China National Space Administration, are working toward sending astronauts to Mars, perhaps by the year 2030. But first they want to find out more about conditions on Mars by sending more probes. In the meantime, astronauts aboard the International Space Station are finding out about the effects of staying in space for long periods. There is a good chance that astronauts will live on Mars one day.

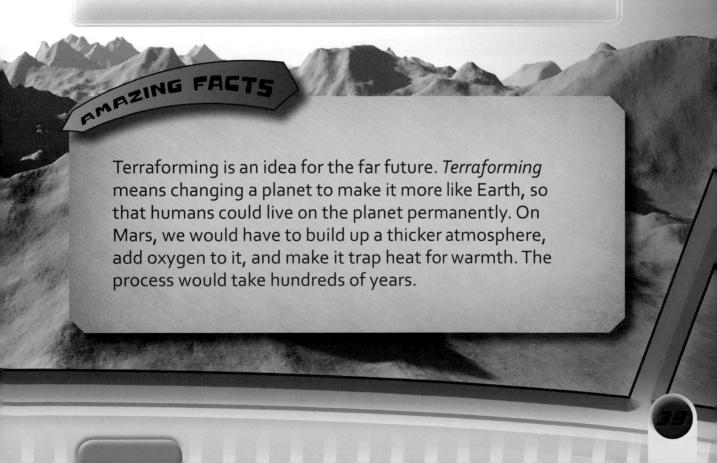

AMAZING FACTS

Terraforming is an idea for the far future. *Terraforming* means changing a planet to make it more like Earth, so that humans could live on the planet permanently. On Mars, we would have to build up a thicker atmosphere, add oxygen to it, and make it trap heat for warmth. The process would take hundreds of years.

MAP OF THE SOLAR SYSTEM

MERCURY

VENUS

EARTH

MARS

ASTEROID BELT

JUPITER

SATURN

URANUS

NEPTUNE

The sizes of the planets and their distances from the Sun are not to scale. To show all the planets' real distances from the Sun, this page would have to be over half a mile long!

TIMELINE

c. 2000 BCE
The Babylonians give the name Nergal to Mars.

1500s
Danish astronomer Tycho Brahe makes careful observations of how Mars moves.

1600s
German astronomer Johannes Kepler figures out the orbit of Mars.
Astronomers, including Galileo Galilei, observe Mars through telescopes.
Christiaan Huygens discovers that Mars spins once every 24 hours.

1877
Italian astronomer Giovanni Schiaparelli makes sketches of channels on Mars.
U.S. astronomer Asaph Hall discovers the moons of Mars and names them Phobos and Deimos.

1965
Mariner 4 is the first probe to arrive at Mars and take photographs.

1971
Mariner 9 is the first spacecraft to go into orbit around Mars.

1976
Viking 1 and *Viking 2* land on Mars to search for signs of life.

2001
Mars Odyssey finds evidence of water near the poles of Mars.

2004
The rovers *Spirit* and *Opportunity* land on Mars.

2011
Astronauts practice a mission to Mars on Earth in the MARS-500 project.

2011
Mars Curiosity is launched, heading for Mars to collect rock samples.

FACT FILE

DIAMETER:
4,220 miles
(6,792 kilometers)

MASS:
10 percent of Earth's mass

AVERAGE DISTANCE FROM SUN:
142 million miles
(228 million kilometers)

NEAREST DISTANCE FROM SUN:
129 million miles
(208 million kilometers)

FURTHEST DISTANCE FROM SUN:
155 million miles
(249 million kilometers)

YEAR LENGTH (THE TIME IT TAKES FOR ONE ORBIT OF THE SUN):
687 Earth days

DAY LENGTH:
24.6 hours

NEAREST DISTANCE FROM EARTH:
35 million miles
(56 million kilometers)

FURTHEST DISTANCE FROM EARTH:
250 million miles
(400 million kilometers)

AVERAGE SURFACE TEMPERATURE:
–82 degrees Fahrenheit
(–63 degrees Celsius)

GRAVITY ON SURFACE:
0.38 times Earth gravity

MOONS:
2 (Phobos and Deimos)

FIRST SPACE PROBE TO VISIT MARS:
Mars 1 (1963)
(first successful probe:
Mariner 4, in 1965)

FIRST MARS LANDER:
Viking 1 (1976)

FIRST MARS ROVER:
Sojourner (1997)

GLOSSARY

astronomer person who studies space

atmosphere layer of gases that surrounds a planet

axis line through a planet or moon that the planet or moon spins around. It always goes through the planet or moon's poles.

canyon valley with very steep or vertical sides

channel long, narrow hole

crater dish-shaped hole in the surface of a planet, made by a meteorite smashing into the surface

diameter distance from one side of a circle or sphere to the other

equator imaginary line around the middle of a planet, halfway between its poles

European Space Agency (ESA) European organization involved in space research and exploration

fossil remains of an animal or plant that died thousands or millions of years ago, found in rock

gravity force that pulls objects toward each other. Big objects, such as planets, have much stronger gravity than smaller objects, such as people.

hemisphere half of a planet

ice cap area of ice-covered land or sea

International Space Station space station with a crew and run by several countries that is orbiting Earth

lander spacecraft that lands on the surface of a planet or moon

mass measure of the amount of material that makes up an object

meteorite piece of rock from space that hits the surface of a planet or moon

microorganism living thing too small to see with the naked eye

NASA short for "National Aeronautics and Space Administration," the U.S. space agency

optical illusion when a person's eyes and brain trick him or her into seeing something that is not there

orbit go around and around a planet or moon

pole two regions at the north and south ends of a planet

probe robot spacecraft sent to visit planets, moons, and other objects in the solar system

radiation particles and rays that come from some objects in space, such as stars. Some types are harmful to humans.

rover robot machine that moves around on wheels or tracks

solar system the Sun, the planets that orbit around the Sun, their moons, and other objects that orbit the Sun, such as asteroids and comets

space station spacecraft in orbit around Earth all the time, which astronauts and scientists visit

telescope device that makes distant objects look bigger

water vapor gas form of water

zero gravity used to describe conditions where there is such a tiny amount of gravity that it makes people weightless, so they float around

FIND OUT MORE

BOOKS

Bond, Peter. *DK Guide to Space* (DK Guides). New York: Dorling Kindersley, 2006.

Goldsmith, Mike. *Solar System* (Discover Science). New York: Macmillan, 2010.

Hartman, Eve, and Wendy Meshbesher. *Mission to Mars* (Science Missions). Chicago: Raintree, 2011.

Oxlade, Chris. *Mercury, Mars, and the Other Inner Planets* (Earth and Space). New York: Rosen Central, 2008.

INTERNET SITES

FactHound offers a safe, fun way to find internet sites related to this book. All of the sites on FactHound have been researched by our staff.

Here's all you do:

Visit *www.facthound.com*

Type in this code: 9781410945709

DVDS

Five Years on Mars (National Geographic, 2010)—a film
about the Mars rovers *Spirit* and *Opportunity*
The Universe (A&E, 2010)

PLACES TO VISIT

Hayden Planetarium
Central Park West and 79th Street, New York, N.Y. 10024
www.haydenplanetarium.org

Kennedy Space Center
SR 405, Kennedy Space Center, Florida 32899
www.nasa.gov/centers/kennedy

Smithsonian National Air and Space Museum
Independence Ave. at 7th St. SW, Washington, D.C. 20560
www.nasm.si.edu

FURTHER RESEARCH

Here are some starting points for finding out more
about Mars:

- Find an online planetarium and see if Mars is visible
  in the night sky.
- Find out more about the lives of early astronomers
  such as Johannes Kepler and Tycho Brahe.
- Find out how telescopes work.
- Follow the progress of the latest missions of probes
  to Mars.
- Find out about living in zero gravity.

INDEX